TV FACTS
AND TRIVIA

by
Alan Lane

SANTA MONICA PRESS
P.O. Box 1076
Santa Monica, CA 90406-1076
Printed in the United States
All Rights Reserved

CONTENTS

Appendix

TEST YOUR KNOWLEDGE OF TV TRIVIA

PART ONE:
ACTORS
AND ACTRESSES

(Answers begin on page 42)

1) What famous actor who portrayed Dustin Hoffman's father in *The Graduate* played the voice of KITT on "Knight Rider"?

2) What soap star played the voice of Charlie on "Charlie's Angels"?

3) Which Monty Python alumnus created and starred in the hilarious comedy "Fawlty Towers," about a husband and wife who run a small hotel?

4) Who was the only cast member of "Gilligan's Island" not invited by producers to reprise her role for the short-lived "Return to Gilligan's Island"?

5) Which two "Diff'rent Strokes" stars have been sent to prison for commiting felonies?

6) Which "Mary Tyler Moore" co-star went on to play the captain on "The Love Boat"?

7) What actor left "M*A*S*H" to play a radio talk show host on the dreadful "Hello, Larry"?

8) Which star of the '60s hit comedy "I Dream of Jeannie" went on to star as J.R. Ewing in "Dallas"?

9) Which actor caused the demise of "Mork and Mindy" by demanding too much money from producers?

10) Which co-star of "The Odd Couple" left the show in order to play Al, the diner owner with the large nose, on "Happy Days"?

11) What dancing movie star played Bandit, the leader of a law-enforcing gang, in the short-lived "Renegades"?

12) Which star of "The Andy Griffith Show" went on to play a garbage collector who builds a rocket in "Salvage 1"?

13) Which "Cheers" actor, whose character is in love with his own hair, is actually balding?

14) Which star of "Barney Miller" died during the show's run?

15) Which star of "Eight is Enough" suffered from an undiagnosed illness for many years and almost died while in a coma?

16) Which star of "Three's Company" has posed nude in *Playboy* twice?

17) Who was the only actor on "Magnum, P.I." who spoke with a fake accent?

18) Which actor on "McHale's Navy" played Murray in "The Mary Tyler Moore Show"?

19) Which star of "Welcome Back, Kotter" became one of the biggest movie stars of the 1970s?

20) What two actors played Father Mulcahey on "M*A*S*H"?

21) Which star of "One Day at a Time" used to take cocaine with her father?

22) Which star of "The Partridge Family" has a brother who starred in "The Hardy Boys"?

23) Which "M*A*S*H" star played hotel manager Lyle Block in "Checking In," a spin-off from "The Jeffersons" that only aired three times?

24) Which star of "Hawaii Five-O" played Felix Lighter, the CIA agent, in *Dr. No*, the first James Bond film?

25) What famous actor/comedian played Jodie, the homosexual, on "Soap"?

26) Which star of "Combat," a show about World War II infantrymen that aired during the 60's, was killed while making *Twilight Zone, the Movie*?

27) Which star of "The Munsters" also starred in "Car 54, Where are You?".

28) What was the name of the dolphin who played Flipper?

29) Which star of "All in the Family" went on to become a successful film director?

30) Which leading actress from "Laverne and Shirley" had appeared occasionally in "The Odd Couple" as Myrna?

31) Which star of "Fantasy Island" played Kahn, the villain, in *Star Trek II, The Wrath of Kahn*?

32) Who was the last member of the original group of "Saturday Night Live" performers cast? Hint: producers feared that his outrageous humor would offend audiences.

33) Which star of "Star Trek" landed his role after turning down the lead in "Dr. Kildare"?

34) Which star of "Get Smart" made her TV debut in 1957, winning the top prize on "The $64,000 Question"?

35) Which star of TV's "Batman" appeared in the Three Stooges' final film?

36) Which star of "The Addams Family" earned an Oscar nomination for a brief appearance in *The Bachelor Party* in 1956?

37) What movie star-turned-director got his first big break as Rowdy Yates on "Rawhide"?

38) What star of Disney's *Zorro* played the role of John Robinson in "Lost in Space"?

39) Which star of "The Honeymooners" made a living as a pool shark before breaking into show business?

40) Which star of "M*A*S*H" was an ardent supporter of the feminist movement, having been cured of a childhood case of polio by a female physician?

41) What famed actor/producer/director was originally chosen to introduce the stories on Rod Serling's "Twilight Zone"?

42) What recurrent character on "Late Night With David Letterman" is played by Calvert de Forest?

43) What British actor created controversy when he chose to play a Russian spy working for the U.S. in "The Man from U.N.C.L.E.," a show which aired during the Cold War years of 1964-1968?

44) Which star of "Mr. Ed" was hailed by *TV Guide* as the Charlie Chaplin of television?

45) What two actors played Darrin Stevens on "Bewitched"?

46) Which star of "Leave it to Beaver" went on to appear in the soap opera "Never Too Young"?

47) Name all 7 hosts of "The Tonight Show."

48) What comedian was the first black performer to star in a dramatic series on American TV?

49) What two actors performed the first interracial kiss on American TV?

50) Who played Tom Willis on "The Jeffersons," a white man with a black wife?

51) Which star of "Gilligan's Island" and "The Many Loves of Dobie Gillis" once taught math and history in elementary school?

52) What "Star Trek" actor played Robin on "Mission: Impossible"?

53) Which star of "Starsky and Hutch" made headlines during the '80s for beating his wife?

54) Which Monkee originally intended to be a jockey?

55) Which two actors on "Taxi" appeared in the film *One Flew Over the Cukoo's Nest*?

56) Which actor from "Gilligan's Island" appeared briefly on "Dynasty"?

57) Which star of "I Love Lucy" dropped out of high school at the age of fifteen?

58) Who played the naughty old man who continually tormented Ruth Buzzi on a park bench in "Rowan and Martin's Laugh-In"?

59) Which star of TV's "Superman" played one of Scarlett's suitors in the classic *Gone with the Wind*?

60) Which actor on "WKRP in Cincinnati" went on to star as a teacher in "Head of the Class"?

61) Which star of "My Sister Sam" was killed by a crazed fan shortly after completing the film *Scenes from the Class Struggle in Beverly Hills*?

62) Which star of "I Spy" played intense FBI agent Bill Maxwell on "The Greatest American Hero"?

63) What real-life recovering alcoholic played the alcoholic police chief on "Hill Street Blues"?

64) Which star of "The Rockford Files" appeared in "Circus Boy," a show that starred Monkee Mickey Dolenz?

65) Which star of "M*A*S*H" left the show because he didn't like working on the outdoor sets?

66) Who was the only American to star in "Monty Python's Flying Circus"?

67) Who was the announcer on both "Dragnet" and Groucho Marx's "You Bet Your Life"?

68) Who hosted every episode of "The Twilight Zone"?

69) What fervent McCarthyist (who almost ruined Lucille Ball by accusing her of being a Communist) was the announcer on "The Untouchables"?

70) What famous comedian played twins Garth and Barth Gimble on the cult-classic "Mary Hartman, Mary Hartman"?

TEST YOUR KNOWLEDGE OF TV TRIVIA

PART TWO: SHOWS
(Answers begin on page 45)

1) The characters in what show lived at 1313 Mockingbird Lane in Mockingbird Heights?

2) What police show featured Howard, the gun-loving head of a SWAT team?

3) "The Six Million Dollar Man" was based on what novel by Martin Caidin?

4) The sitcom "Alice" was based on what Academy award-winning film by Martin Scorsese?

5) What '60s variety show frequently came under fire because its two stars continually defied network censors?

6) What popular comedy show featured a theme song entitled "Suicide is Painless"?

7) Name all four spin-offs from "All in the Family."

8) What was the first cartoon ever to be aired during prime time?

9) What contemporary TV show became more popular than ever when certain viewers tried to ban it for its tasteless view of marriage?

10) What show featured a harpsicord playing butler named Lurch?

11) David Carradine starred as Caine, the Amerasian martial artist who lived in the Old West, in what show?

12) What comedy show made the line "Sock it to me" famous?

13) What show centered on a group of spies devoted to defeating THRUSH, an international criminal cartel?

14) What Norman Lear comedy starring Louise Lasser was the first show ever to satirize soap operas, as well as one of the most controversial programs of the '70s?

15) What show regularly featured rate-a-record segments and Clearasil commercials?

16) What 1950's show featured an accountant, the perfect mother, and their two sons living at 485 Maple Drive in Mayfield?

17) What dramatic series starring Pernel Roberts was a spin-off from "M*A*S*H"?

18) What show took place in the Old West and featured stories about spies and nuclear weapons?

19) What show starred Lee Majors and Heather Thomas as stunt-people?

20) What show featured a special guest villain each week?

21) Chuck Connors starred as Lucas McCain in what Cold War-allegory Western?

22) What police show took place in the squad room of the 12th Precinct in Greenwich Village, New York?

23) Forrest Tucker and Larry Storch starred in what 1975 comedy about paranormal investigators (the title of which was later used in a popular movie)?

24) What action series centered around a group of spies who worked for IMF, the espionage branch of an unidentified government agency?

25) What politically charged cartoon featured Boris and Natasha, Mr. Peabody and Sherman, Dudley Doright, and Mr. Know-It-All?

26) What acclaimed ABC news program originally aired as a means of keeping Americans informed about the hostages taken in Iran?

27) What classic sitcom revolved around the people working at the WJM newsroom?

28) What morning news show features popular weatherman Willard Scott?

29) What show launched the careers of the Not-Ready-for-Prime-Time players?

30) What interview show starring Tom Snyder used to air on NBC at the time currently occupied by "Late Night With David Letterman"?

31) What show featured Sgt. Ernie Bilko as the boss of the motor pool in Fort Baxter?

32) What show featured a bus driver and sewer worker who belonged to the Raccoon Lodge?

33) What daytime soap opera featured a vampire, a werewolf, a witch, a monster from another dimension, and a warlock?

34) What cartoon centered around the four-legged residents of Jellystone park?

35) What comedy show about a group of transit workers had such a talented cast that they were all nominated for a Golden Globe award in 1979?

36) What long-running variety show originally went by the name "Toast of the Town"?

37) What show starred four young musicians who were "just trying to be friendly"?

38) What dramatic cop show took place in the 13th Precinct in New York?

39) What quiz show did Merv Griffin re-create?

40) What military sitcom featured a character who had worked at Wally's filling station?

41) What show featured a boat captain whose full name was Jonas Grumby?

42) Sidney Fields was the landlord of what two comedians?

43) What cop show was about an investigator who had been crippled by an assassination attempt?

44) What was the name of the adventure show about "a big man" with two kids called Jemima and Israel?

45) What show set in rural Jefferson County during the Depression was about an eldest son who hopes to become a writer?

46) What show was about a junkyard owner who pretended to have a heart attack whenever his son said he wanted to leave home?

47) What show centered on the sheriff of Mayberry, North Carolina?

48) What spin-off from "All in the Family" was about a dominating woman married to the owner of Findlay's Friendly Appliances?

49) What sitcom was about two divorced men who lived together and often bickered as if they were a married couple?

50) What light-hearted crime drama was about a detective who lived in a house trailer and ate tacos for breakfast?

51) What show about a con-man and two cabbies was finally taken off the air after viewers protested its obvious racism?

52) What 1960s show was about four World War II commandos who broke away from the American army and fought the war on their own terms?

53) What campy cop show featured a catchy theme song and the inevitable line, "Book 'em, Dan-O"?

54) What show was about a white professional basketball player who becomes a coach at a predominately black school after a knee injury?

55) What sitcom starring Jimmy Walker was about a black family struggling to make it out of the projects?

56) What acclaimed crime drama was about two women investigators fighting crime on the streets and sexism in the police force?

57) What show featured the brave men who rode on Silver and Scout?

58) What show was about a Vietnam commando unit convicted of a crime they did not commit?

59) What short-lived sitcom featured Matt Frewer (aka Max Headroom) as a doctor who gives medical advice on TV and writes trashy romance novels in his spare time?

60) What sitcom was about a high school student who hoped to become a journalist and earned his money as a DJ for WOW radio?

61) What new name was given to "Valerie" when producers decided to fire star Valerie Harper?

62) What short-lived adventure show about young computer hackers tried to cash in on the success of *Wargames*?

63) What radio station broadcasts from Suite 1412 of the Flem building?

64) What police show is about a sergeant on the L.C.P.D. who holds the record for the most squad cars damaged during high speed chases?

65) On what show did the Blues Brothers make their TV debut?

66) What wonderful children's show featured such memorable characters as Bunny Rabbit, Mr. Greenjeans, and Grandfather Clock?

TEST YOUR KNOWLEDGE OF TV TRIVIA

PART THREE: CHARACTERS

(Answers on page 48)

1) What was the full name of the Professor on "Gilligan's Island"?

2) What was Meathead's real name on "All in the Family"?

3) Who was the Daily Planet's cub reporter on "Superman"?

4) What was the name of Jed Clampett's thick-headed nephew on "The Beverly Hillbillies"?

5) Who was the top agent working for U.N.C.L.E. in "The Man from U.N.C.L.E."?

6) Name all of the members of "The Addams Family."

7) Who was the frustrated district attorney who lost a court case against Perry Mason in every episode but one?

8) Not including Max, who was the stupidest agent in CONTROL on "Get Smart"?

9) What character on "Star Trek" was in love with Mr. Spock, the half-human, half-Vulcan science officer of the Enterprise?

10) Name all three of John Steed's female sidekicks in "The Avengers."

11) What was Patrick McGoohan's designation in "The Prisoner"?

12) What was the name of Dobie's best friend, the beatnik, on "The Many Loves of Dobie Gillis"?

13) Which of the "Three Stooges" were actually related to each other?

14) Who were the three "Maverick" brothers?

15) Who was the small-time con-man that Jim often relied on in "The Rockford Files"?

16) Who did Bamboo Harvester play on "The Mr. Ed Show"?

17) Who was Samantha Stevens' witch doctor on "Bewitched"?

18) Who were Sgt. Joe Friday's two longest running partners on "Dragnet"?

19) Who was Eddie Haskell's best friend on "Leave it to Beaver"?

20) What was the name of the dwarf who hoped to blow up the world on "The Wild, Wild West"?

21) What was Batman's real name on the show?

22) What was the name of the eccentric right-wing inspector who constantly disturbed the squad room detectives in "Barney Miller"?

23) Who was the delicious fashion model working for the Impossible Mission Force in "Mission: Impossible"?

24) Who did Boris Badenov and Natasha Fatale work for in "The Adventures of Rocky and Bullwinkle"?

25) Who was the only character not fired from the station when "Mary Tyler Moore" came to an end?

26) What family of disfigured aliens lived in suburban America and told all their visitors that they were from France on "Saturday Night Live"?

27) Which character on "Dark Shadows" wanted to make a race of soldiers for Satan?

28) B.J. Hunnicut's full first name on "M*A*S*H" was revealed to be what?

29) What was Ralph Kramden's job on "The Honeymooners"?

30) On "Taxi", "Reverend" Jim changed his last name to Ignatausky because he thought it would spell what backwards?

31) Which "Monkees" character was so popular that a young British singer who had the same name had to change it to David Bowie?

32) What was Mary Anne's last name on "Gilligan's Island"?

33) Whose philosophy on life was "Nip it in the bud!" on "The Andy Griffith Show"?`

34) What "fast" companion did Oscar and Felix usually invite over on poker night in "The Odd Couple"?

35) What character on "Fawlty Towers" was the constant target of Basil Fawlty's wrath?

36) Which character on "Space: 1999" was a shape-shifting alien?

37) Which character on "Hill Street Blues" was constantly interrupted by phone calls from his mother?

38) Which character on "Cheers" held the record for being hit on the head the most times with a baseball?

39) Which mohawked member of "The A-Team" was afraid to fly?

40) Which character's Indian name on "The Lone Ranger" translated to faithful friend?

41) What was Colt Seaver's occupation on the action series "The Fall Guy"?

42) What was the name of Bob Newhart's character on "The Bob Newhart Show", and what was the name of his character on "Newhart"?

43) What was Jack Tripper's occupation on "Three's Company"?

44) Which two partners on "Hill Street Blues" were shot and almost killed on the first episode after their squad car was stolen in a bad part of town?

45) Who was the first dog in history ever to adopt a little boy, and then go on to build a time machine, in "The Adventures of Rocky and Bullwinkle"?

46) What two famous prehistoric families resided in the town of Bedrock?

47) What was the name of the maid on "The Jeffersons"?

48) What mouse appeared frequently on "The Ed Sullivan Show"?

49) Which character on "Hogan's Heroes" was a chef from France?

50) Name the three owners of "Arnold's" on "Happy Days."

51) Which character ran the "Long Branch Saloon" on "Gunsmoke"?

52) What short-lived character on "Taxi" was studying to be a park ranger?

53) Christopher George played what sargeant on "The Rat Patrol"?

54) Who is John Ross better known as on "Dallas"?

55) Name the first four Sweathogs featured on "Welcome Back, Kotter."

56) What did Ward Cleaver do for a living on "Leave it to Beaver"?

57) What character was Eddie Murphy playing when he made his TV debut on "Saturday Night Live"?

58) Who were the first three residents on the Swamp on "M*A*S*H"?

59) What was James Kirk's middle name on "Star Trek"?

60) John Schneider and Tom Wopat played what two cousins on "The Dukes of Hazard"?

61) What was the name of the commander of the "Battlestar Galactica"?

ANSWERS
TO TV TRIVIA
QUESTIONS

ACTORS AND ACTRESSES

1) William Daniels
2) John Forsythe
3) John Cleese
4) Tina Louise (Ginger Grant)
5) Dana Plato (Kimberly), for armed robbery; Todd Bridges (Willis), for attempted murder
6) Gavin MacLeod (Murray)
7) McLean Stevenson (Henry Blake)
8) Larry Hagman
9) Pam Dawber (Mindy)
10) Al Molinaro
11) Patrick Swayze
12) Andy Griffith
13) Ted Danson (Sam Malone)
14) Jack Soo (Nick Yemana)
15) Adam Rich (Nicholas Bradford)
16) Suzanne Sommers
17) John Hillerman (Higgins) is not really British
18) Gavin MacLeod
19) John Travolta (Vinnie Barbarino)
20) George Morgan and William Christopher
21) Mackenzie Phillips (Julie)
22) David Cassidy (Keith Partridge); his brother Shaun Cassidy played Joe Hardy

23) Larry Linville
24) Jack Lord
25) Billy Crystal
26) Vic Morrow
27) Fred Gwynne (Herman Munster)
28) Suzy
29) Rob Reiner
30) Penny Marshall
31) Ricardo Mantalban
32) John Belushi
33) William Shatner
34) Barbara Feldon (Agent 99)
35) Adam West (Batman)
36) Carolyn Jones (Morticia Addams)
37) Clint Eastwood
38) Guy Williams
39) Jackie Gleason (Ralph Kramden)
40) Alan Alda (Hawkeye Pierce)
41) Orson Welles
42) Larry "Bud" Melman
43) David McCallum (Illya Kuryakin)
44) Alan Young (Wilbur Post)
45) Dick York and Dick Sargent
46) Tony Dow
47) Steve Allen, Ernie Kovacks, Jack Lescoulie, Al "Jazzbo" Collins, Jack Paar, Johnny Carson, and Jay Leno

48) Bill Cosby (Alexander Scott in "I Spy")
49) William Shatner and Nichelle Nichols (in "Star Trek")
50) Franklin Cover
51) Bob Denver
52) Leonard Nimoy
53) David Soul
54) Davy Jones
55) Danny DeVito and Christopher Lloyd
56) Tina Louise (Ginger Grant)
57) Lucille Ball
58) Arte Johnson
59) George Reeves (Superman)
60) Howard Hesseman (Dr. Johnny Fever)
61) Rebecca Schaeffer (Patti Russell)
62) Robert Culp
63) Daniel J. Travanti
64) Noah Beery ("Rocky" Rockford)
65) McLean Stevenson (Henry Blake)
66) Terry Gilliam
67) George Fenneman
68) Rod Serling
69) Walter Winchell
70) Martin Mull

SHOWS

1) "The Munsters"
2) "Hill Street Blues"
3) "Cyborg"
4) *Alice Doesn't Live Here Anymore*
5) "The Smothers Brothers Comedy Hour"
6) "M*A*S*H"
7) "Maude," "The Jeffersons," "Archie Bunker's Place," and "Gloria"
8) "The Flintstones"
9) "Married with Children"
10) "The Addams Family"
11) "Kung Fu"
12) "Laugh-In"
13) "The Man from U.N.C.L.E."
14) "Mary Hartman, Mary Hartman"
15) "American Bandstand"
16) "Leave it to Beaver"
17) "Trapper John, MD"
18) "The Wild, Wild West"
19) "The Fall Guy"
20) "Batman"
21) "The Rifleman"
22) "Barney Miller"
23) "Ghost Busters"
24) "Mission: Impossible"

25) "The Adventures of Bullwinkle and Rocky"
26) "Nightline"
27) "The Mary Tyler Moore Show"
28) "The Today Show"
29) "Saturday Night Live"
30) "Tomorrow"
31) "The Phil Silvers Show"
32) "The Honeymooners"
33) "Dark Shadows"
34) "Yogi Bear"
35) "Taxi"
36) "The Ed Sullivan Show"
37) "The Monkees"
38) "Kojak"
39) "Jeopardy"
40) "Gomer Pyle, USMC"
41) "Gilligan's Island"
42) "Abbott and Costello"
43) "Ironside"
44) "Daniel Boone"
45) "The Waltons"
46) "Sanford and Son"
47) "The Andy Griffith Show"
48) "Maude"
49) "The Odd Couple"
50) "The Rockford Files"

51) "Amos 'n' Andy"
52) "Rat Patrol"
53) "Hawaii Five-O"
54) "The White Shadow"
55) "Good Times"
56) "Cagney and Lacey"
57) "The Lone Ranger"
58) "The A-Team"
59) "Doctor, Doctor"
60) "Happy Days"
61) "The Hogan Family"
62) "The Whiz Kids"
63) "WKRP in Cincinatti"
64) "T.J. Hooker"
65) "Saturday Night Live"
66) "Captain Kangaroo"

CHARACTERS

1) Roy Hinkley
2) Mike Stivic
3) Jimmy Olsen
4) Jethro Bodine
5) Napoleon Solo
6) Gomez, Morticia, Pugsley, Wednesday, Uncle Fester, Grandmama, Cousin Itt, Thing, and Lurch
7) Hamilton Burger
8) Larrabee
9) Nurse Christine Chapel
10) Cathy Gale, Emma Peel, Linda Thorson
11) Number 6
12) Maynard G. Krebs
13) Moe, Curly, and Shemp
14) Bret, Bart, and Brent
15) Angel Martin
16) Mr. Ed
17) Dr. Bombay
18) Frank Smith (1953-59) and Bill Gannon (1967-69)
19) Lumpy Rutherford
20) Dr. Miguelito Loveless
21) Bruce Wayne
22) Inspector Luger

23) Cinnamon Carter
24) Fearless Leader
25) Ted Baxter
26) The Coneheads
27) Nicholas Blair
28) B.J.
29) Bus driver
30) Starchild
31) Davy Jones
32) Summers
33) Barney Fife
34) Speed
35) Manuel
36) Maya
37) Belker "the Biter"
38) Coach
39) BA Baracus
40) The Lone Ranger ("Kimo Sabe")
41) Stunt man
42) Bob Hartley and Dick Louden
43) Chef
44) Hill and Renko
45) Mr. Peabody
46) The Flintstones and the Rubbles
47) Florence
48) Topo Gigio
49) LeBeau

50) Arnold, Al, and Fonzie
51) Miss Kitty
52) John Burns
53) Sargeant Sam Troy
54) J.R. Ewing
55) Barbarino, Washington, Epstein, and Horschack
56) Accountant
57) Little Richard Simmons
58) Hawkeye, Trapper, and Frank
59) Tiberius
60) Bo and Luke Duke
61) Adama

FASCINATING FACTS ABOUT YOUR FAVORITE TV SHOWS

THE ADDAMS FAMILY

The show was based on a comic strip featured in *The New Yorker*.

None of the characters had first names in the comic strip. The producers quickly had to devise names for them. Gomez was almost called Repelli, short for repellent.

Jackie Coogan, the child star who had become a sensation by playing the title role in Chaplin's classic *The Kid*, played bald Uncle Fester. Coogan was worth millions as a child, but his mother had spent his entire trust fund before he ever saw any of it. He subsequently turned to a life of drugs, finally returning to the screen for "The Addams Family."

Pugsley was played by Ken Weatherwax, the nephew of Lassie's trainer.

Carolyn Jones (Morticia) got the part because she was a rising star, and the network insisted on at least one well-known actor in the show. She had to wear plenty of make-up for the part, including a wig of actual human hair.

The butler Lurch was played by first time actor Ted Cassidy. He went on to perform such classic roles as Bigfoot in "The Six Million Dollar Man" and the voice of "The Hulk."

Ted Cassidy also usually played Thing, the hand in a box. Thing was almost always a right hand, but Cassidy occasionally used his left to see if anyone would notice.

The only reason the network picked up the show was because they wanted to compete against another network's highly successful "The Munsters."

The show was lauded by the PTA for its non-violence.

ALL IN THE FAMILY

This show was based on the British series "Til Death Do Us Part." "All in the Family" was originally named "Those were the Days" by producers.

"All in the Family" was one of the raciest shows ever to appear on American TV. It dealt with issues that TV still has trouble handling today. Rape, bigotry, urban crime and poverty, and politics were all grappled with in this show.

At one point during the show's run, producers were having difficulty renegotiating Carroll O'Connor's (Archie Bunker) contract. As a result, they were going to have Archie killed by a mugger if O'Connor refused to sign another contract.

Mike "Meathead" Stivic (Archie's liberal son-in-law) was played by Rob Reiner. He is the son of comedian Carl Reiner, and he is currently a successful film director.

This show had four direct spin-offs: "Maude," "The Jeffersons," "Archie Bunker's Place," and "Gloria."

The storylines of each episode dealt very directly with current events. In one episode, for example, Meathead and Archie are voting for different Presidential candidates (they were the actual Democratic and Republican candidates for that year). The whole episode was essentially a debate over the strengths and weaknesses of each candidate.

Famous lines from the show: "You knuckle-head!" and "Aaaaaaarchieeeeeeee."

Archie was continually challenged to reassess his bigoted values. When his best friend dies, Archie learns for the first time that he was Jewish. He almost decides not to attend the funeral, but he finally makes the right decision, and he even delivers the eulogy.

THE ANDY GRIFFITH SHOW

This show was a spin-off from "The Danny Thomas Show."

Ronny Howard played Andy's son Opie. Howard's father had to be on the set with him, as he was only six years old. Whenever the young actor would become difficult to work with, his father would spank him. Howard quickly became very amenable to the rest of the cast and crew. He has since gone on to star in "Happy Days" and direct several feature films.

Jack Nicholson guest starred in two episodes of the show.

The whistled theme tune to the show is called *The Fishing Hole*. Lyrics were recorded to go with the music, but they were never used.

Andy Griffith had been discovered by a record executive who heard his stand-up routine while travelling through the South. The executive signed him to a contract, and he was soon starring in films such as *No Time for Sergeants* which made him a star. When his status on the silver screen began to fade, he decided to switch to TV.

Don Knotts (Barney Fife) had worked on Broadway with Andy Griffith. He was out of work when the show debuted, so he asked if he could play the part of a deputy. Griffith agreed, and Knotts went on to win five Emmies.

Jim Nabors played Gomer Pyle. Pyle was such a well-received character that producers gave him his own show: "Gomer Pyle, USMC." This show had some of the best ratings of the sixties. Prior to acting, Nabors received a degree in business administration and worked in the United Nations.

BARNEY MILLER

This is one of the most respected shows of all time. The New York Police Department made honorary detectives out of each of the stars. Los Angeles mayor Tom Bradley once declared a Barney Miller week. Parts of the set for the show even reside in the Smithsonian Institute in Washington, DC.

Hal Linden (Barney Miller) had been a struggling actor, musician, and singer for twenty years when he finally got his break in 1971. He won the Tony award for best actor in a musical. He was shortly thereafter cast as Captain Miller, the first Jewish police captain in TV history.

A major reason for the richness and realism of the characters on this show is because they resembled very closely the actors who portrayed them. Producers wanted this to be a show about human issues, so they let the actors mold the characters into themselves, with their own strengths and weaknesses.

The shabby squad room was based on a real squad room the producer once visited. While working on a previous show, he once had to bail his entire crew out of jail for littering.

The original pilot for the show was called "The Life and Times of Barney Miller." It focused more on his home life than on his escapades at work.

Hal Linden had little faith that the show would last more than a few episodes. He didn't even bring his family to California with him when the show began because he figured he would be back home in a few weeks.

Jack Soo (Nick Yemana) had spent most of WWII in a Japanese internment camp. He refused to accept stereotypical roles and, as a result, he found very little work. The producer of the show was his good friend, and he offered Soo the role because he realized he could bring humanity and warmth to it.

Max Gail (Wojohowicz) had worked as a prison guard prior to starring in the show.

BATMAN

This show featured such famous guest stars as Cesar Romero, Eartha Kitt, Burgess Meredith, John Astin, Julie Newmar, Frank Gorshin, Joan Collins, Vincent Price, Milton Berle, Cliff Robertson, and Liberace.

The character of Aunt Harriet was added to the show by producers (she was never in the comic books) in order to avoid any charges of homosexuality levied against the show. An old butler, a young boy, and a bachelor millionaire seemed like an odd trio to be living alone in stately Wayne manor.

The show's cheesy sets were much more expensive to make than one might think. The batcave, for example, cost over $800,000.

The network once interrupted the show with a special news report about an emergency landing of Gemini 8. They received thousands of calls from angry batfans demanding to know the outcome of the episode.

The only member of the cast ever to receive an Emmy nomination was Frank Gorshin, for his performance of the Riddler.

The amazing Batmobile was nothin more than a modified Lincoln Continental. The costs for the modification ran $30,000)

Alfred was the only character to know the identity of the Dynamic Duo and Batgirl.

The show featured some of the most absurd crimes of all time. The Joker once turned Gotham City's water supply into jelly, for example.

Adam West (Batman) appeared in the Three Stooge's final movie.

Burt Ward (Robin) was a real estate broker prior to starring in the show. He was so bad at it, however, that he only ever sold two houses.

Batman was the first comic book superhero show to be broadcast during prime time in the 1960s.

BEWITCHED

As many viewers are aware, two different actors played Darrin. Dick York, the first Darrin, had injured his back in 1959 while making a film with Gary Cooper. His condition worsened through the years, and he finally had to leave the show. He was replaced by Dick Sargent, a similar looking actor.

Elizabeth Montgomery (Samantha) was eight months pregnant when the show started filming. As a result, she was unable to be on the set for the first five episodes. Directors shot these episodes without her, and then they filmed her parts as soon as she was able to come back to work. Quite a change from the days of live TV.

Samantha's daughter on the show was named Tabitha. Because of the popularity of the show, thousands of newborn girls were named after her.

Samantha's mother Endora (Agnes Moorhead) only calls Darrin by his real name in one episode. In every other episode she purposely mispronounces it: Durwood, Dobbin, Dum-Dum, Darwin, Donald, Dumbo.

Agnes Moorhead had made her screen debut in Orson Welles' legendary *Citizen Kane*. Regrettably, the popularity of "Bewitched" made most viewers forget about the rest of her prestigious career, which included five Oscar nominations.

The show featured several other famous actors in recurring roles. Dr. Bombay, Samantha's "witch doctor," was played by renowned British actor Bernard Fox. Maurice Evans, a famous thespian, played Samantha's father, Maurice. And Paul Lynde (of "Hollywood Squares" fame) played Samantha's Uncle Arthur.

One of the creators of the show, William Dozier, also created the cult classic "Batman."

Dick Sargent (Darrin number two) had never been in a successful TV show, despite appearing in such films as *Operation Petticoat*. Bad luck stayed with him for "Bewitched." As soon as he replaced Dick York, the show's ratings plummetted.

THE BULLWINKLE SHOW

This was the second cartoon series ever to be broadcast during prime time ("The Flintstones" was the first).

The network was constantly infuriated by Jay Ward, the show's creator. He continually pulled off-the-wall stunts in his show. In one episode, he had Bullwinkle tell audience members to pull the knobs off their TV sets so that "we'll be sure to be with you next week." 20,000 kids obliged the request. The following week Bullwinkle told those kids to glue the knobs back on.

"The Bullwinkle Show" was replete with social satire. Kids just didn't get it. As a result, the show did not last very long.

Very few of the shows ever had real scripts. Jay Ward encouraged his voice talents to ad-lib as much as they wanted. This often resulted in episodes that ran too long. Ward's solution to this problem: cut out as much of the plot as necessary in order to keep all of the jokes in place.

William Conrad (of "Cannon" and "Jake and the Fatman" fame) was the sarcastic narrator of each episode. Who would have guessed?

The closing credits to the show feature between fifty and one hundred names. But in reality the whole show was made by fewer than a dozen people. Jay Ward simply felt the credits would look silly if they only contained twelve names.

Famous plot from one episode of "The Bullwinkle Show": The world economy is based on cereal box tops and the evil Boris Badenov intends to throw the world into chaos by counterfeiting them.

Famous line from every episode: "Rocky, watch me pull a rabbit outta my hat...Whoops. Wrong hat."

This show turned every convention upside down. Instead of telling stories about a boy who has a dog, Jay Ward told stories about a dog who has a boy. The dog was even a genius inventor who made a time machine called the WABAC machine.

CHEERS

The bar in the show is based on an actual tavern called "The Bull and Finch."

The creators of this show were the same people who produced "Taxi." Rhea Perlman (Carla) and Ted Danson (Sam) had both also appeared on "Taxi."

This was one of the first comedies to deal seriously with issues that became prominent in the eighties: alcoholism, working women, tensions over sexual relationships.

Kelsey Grammer (Frasier Crane) has been arrested several times for possession of cocaine.

Ted Danson debuted on TV in a short lived soap named "Somerset."

Shelley Long (Diane) left the show because of her bad relations with the other cast members.

GET SMART

The 1960s marked a craze in spy-related entertainment. "Get Smart" was not only the first parody of a spy show, but also one of the most successful parodies of all time. It won seven Emmies and sustained extremely high ratings.

The show was created by comedy greats Mel Brooks (B*lazing Saddles*) and Buck Henry (*The Graduate, Catch-22*).

Agent 99 (Barbara Feldon) was never given a name on the show. She went by Susan Hilton in one episode, but this was later revealed to be a cover.

Don Adams (Maxwell Smart) had a successful stand-up comedy routine which relied heavily on impersonations of famous actors. This came in very handy for "Get Smart." The voice he used for Smart was his impersonation of William Powell in *The Thin Man*.

Max's cover was as a greeting card salesman for the Pontiac Greeting Card Company.

Barbara Feldon once won the top prize on "The $64,000 Question." She answered questions about Shakespeare.

Edward Platt (the Chief) studied as an opera singer at Juliard. He met Jose Ferrer on Broadway, who helped him break into film. His most famous role is as James Dean's juvenile officer in *Rebel Without a Cause*.

Max's one-liners became favorite slang expressions of the day. Some of these included: "Sorry about that, Chief," "Would you believe," "Missed me by that much," "The old...trick," and "That's the second biggest...I've ever seen."

The network cancelled the show after four seasons. It was promptly picked up by a competing network, but their attempts to revive it failed, and the show went off the air after just one more season.

The show featured such inane gadgets as Max's shoe phone (which would start ringing at inappropriate times) and the cone of silence (in which nobody can hear a word).

GILLIGAN'S ISLAND

The idea behind the show was a remarkably profound one. Producers hoped to create characters symbolic of groups in American society, strand them on an island, and observe their interactions.

The network was concerned that the audience would not understand how the castaways became stranded on the island. As a result, producers wrote the theme song for the show themselves and sang it to network executives. The executives were satisfied.

The island was a man-made body located in the center of a lake in the network's outdoor studio. It cost $75,000 to build it.

"Gilligan's Island" was loved by the public and had incredibly good ratings, despite continual attacks by critics and reviewers. The show was finally cancelled when "Gunsmoke" was moved to its time spot in order to boost its ratings.

All of the actors became very good friends,

except for Tina Louise (Ginger Grant, the movie star). Bob Denver (Gilligan) once even refused to pose for a photograph with her.

Bob Denver had been an elementary school math teacher.

Jim Backus (Thurston Howell, III) agreed to do the part without reading the script because he was a friend of the producer. But when he finally did read the script, he hated it so much that he demanded twice as much money as he had previously been offered.

Some viewers actually sent letters to the US Coast Guard asking them to rescue the castaways.

The pilot film for the show was shot on location in Hawaii. Filming was completed on November 22, 1963 (the day President Kennedy was shot).

Alan Hale (the Skipper) once broke his arm midway through the season. But he did not tell anyone until the season was over, so that the shooting schedule wouldn't be interrupted.

HILL STREET BLUES

This show was created when a network executive came up with the idea "Barney Miller Outside."

This show never had a large audience even though it was one of the most critically acclaimed series of all time. If it had not been broadcast immediately following such popular shows as "The Cosby Show" and "Cheers," it might never have survived.

Two of the stars, Hill (Michael Warren) and Renko (Charles Haid) were killed in the first episode. But the producers liked them so much that they brought them back to life and even considered giving them their own show.

This was the first show with a huge cast and continuing plotlines that rose above mere soap opera status. Its successors include "St. Elsewhere" and "LA Law."

Memorable lines: "Let's be careful out there," and "Hi, Ma."

THE HONEYMOONERS

Jackie Gleason (Ralph Kramden) had been a pool shark by day and a struggling stand-up comic by night. One day he performed his comedy routine while incredibly drunk; he couldn't remember most of his lines, so he just insulted audience members, and his new act was a big success. He was soon hired by Warner Brothers to star in movies and on television.

Gleason was an incredible performer. He never needed to rehearse his part or even study his lines. He would just browse over the script casually before filming began.

The show was made when television was always broadcast live. There was no way to edit out mistakes. If Gleason ever forgot his lines, he would signal a prompt by patting his stomach.

Despite continual popularity today, this show only ran for one season as a half-hour sitcom (there are only 39 episodes). "The Honeymooners" started as a regular sketch on one of

Gleason's prior variety shows, and it continued as such after the series came to an end.

None of the stars of the show (except Audrey Meadows, who played Alice Kramden) receive residual payments from reruns of the show. Unlike today, show business contracts in the fities typically did not foresee repeats. But Audrey Meadows was shrewd enough to make sure she had her bases covered.

Ralph's friend Ed Norton (Art Carney) worked in the sewer. He had plenty of wise sayings from his workplace. For example: "As we say in the sewer, here's mud in your eye." Or: "As we say in the sewer, time and tide wait for no man."

Gleason initially turned down Audrey Meadows for the part of his wife because he thought she was too pretty. She returned wearing no makeup and a poor housewife's dress. Gleason didn't recognize her and hired her immediately.

Famous quotes from the show: "One of these days, Alice...Pow! Right in the kisser!" and "Hiya there, Ralphie boy."

LATE NIGHT
WITH DAVID LETTERMAN

About twelve years ago, Johnny Carson thought about leaving "The Tonight Show." David Letterman was to be his successor. But Johnny decided to stay on, so Letterman got his own show. Since Jay Leno recently became Carson's replacement, Letterman has declared angrily that he might move to a different network.

Letterman lives in Malibu. He commutes to New York to tape the show, and stays at a house in nearby Connecticut.

Paul Schaffer, the band leader, used to play with the band on "Saturday Night Live."

Regular guests on the show include Biff Henderson and Al Maar, two stagehands. Calvert de Forrest (Larry "Bud" Melman) also puts in regular appearances interviewing people on the street.

Memorable gags: "Viewer Mail," and "Top Ten Lists."

I LOVE LUCY

Desi Arnaz was the son of a Cuban senator and a beautiful model. He was born to great wealth, but he was forced to leave his homeland at the age of 16 during the Batista revolution.

Lucille Ball dropped out of high school when she was fifteen so that she could become an actress.

The only reason that Lucille Ball created the show was so that she could mend her faltering marriage to Desi Arnaz by spending more time with him.

William Frawley (Fred Mertz) had such a bad reputation for his heavy drinking that he had to sign a contract saying that he would never show up to the set drunk.

Vivian Vance (Ethel Mertz) hated her character being married to someone so much older.

The only reason that Lucy became pregnant on the show was because she was pregnant in real life. The network insisted the word "expecting" be used on the air instead of "pregnant."

After "I Love Lucy" came to an end, Desi Arnaz produced the show "The Untouchables." Mobsters responded by putting out a contract on his life.

In the age of live broadcasts, "I Love Lucy" was the first TV series ever filmed and subsequently aired at a later date.

During the life of the show, the only other show that ever had higher ratings was "The $64,000 Question."

The network initially rejected Lucille Ball's request for her real husband to play her TV husband. Who would believe it? She threatened to move to another network, so they finally relented.

Dwight D. Eisenhower made the mistake of televising his inauguration during the same time spot as "I Love Lucy." Almost twice as many viewers tuned in to watch her show than to watch him.

LEAVE IT TO BEAVER

On October 4, 1957, "Leave it to Beaver" premiered and Sputnik I was launched. Although these events seem quite unrelated, they set a clear tone for America in the fifties. It looked at the world through rose colored glasses despite standing on the threshold of the Cold War.

The first episode filmed was delayed by network censors because it showed a toilet bowl. The network finally agreed to air it.

The producers of "Leave it to Beaver" also produced "The Munsters." Many stories of the latter show were ripped off directly from "Leave it to Beaver."

The show was originally entitled "Wally and Beaver." It was the first sitcom ever to center around the children rather than the parents.

The only reason that Barbara Billingsley (June Cleaver) wore a pearl necklace in every episode is because she had an extremely thin neck.

Jerry Mathers (the Beaver) was a pin-up boy by the time he was two, appearing in a department store calendar. By the time he was four he had appeared in an Alfred Hitchcock movie. He was cast as the Beaver when he was eight.

Tony Dow (Wally Cleaver) was cast in the role accidentally. He merely accompanied his friend to the auditions, but the producers preferred him.

Ken Osmond played Eddie Haskell, Wally's best friend. He joined the LAPD in 1970 and was decorated for his valor. A rumor once circulated that he was porn star John Holmes.

Although "Leave it to Beaver" is one of the best remembered shows of the 1950s, it was never very successful during its day. It never ranked among the top 25 shows of the year.

Famous lines from the show include: "Gee, Wally," "Boy, Beave, are you gonna get it," and "Ward, I'm very worried about the Beaver."

LOST IN SPACE

The major financier of this show was Groucho Marx.

This was the first science fiction show of the 1960s. It was soon to be followed by such classics as "Star Trek." The show was originally intended to be very serious, but it eventually became quite funny, giving in to the demand for campy humor on TV which was created by "Batman."

Dr. Zachary Smith (Jonathan Harris), the show's bad guy, was originally slated to appear in only six episodes. But he received so much fan mail that producers decided to make him the star, much to the chagrin of Guy Williams (Professor John Robinson), the original star of the show.

The Robot was played by a stuntman who had doubled for Red Buttons. It was designed by Bob Kinoshita, the same man who created Robby the Robot for the classic sci-fi film *Forbidden Planet*.

Billy Mumy played Will, the Robinson's son. His first TV appearance had been on "Romper Room" when he was three.

The two central characters of virtually every episode of the show are Smith and the Robot. Smith's plans to eliminate the Robinsons are constantly thwarted by the Robot.

Famous line: "Danger, Will Robinson! Danger! Danger!"

Famous storyline: The Robot passes through some mysterious marsh gas that turns him into a giant. The Robinsons must go inside him to save him.

Nobody told the cast members that the show had been cancelled. They had to read about it in the newspaper.

MAGNUM, PI

Magnum's boss on the show was never seen. His voice was heard, however. It was supplied by Orson Welles.

This show was broadcast by the same network that produced "Hawaii Five-O." It was even filmed in the same locations and aired during the same time slot as the earlier show.

Tom Selleck had made his debut as an investigator on the acclaimed series "The Rockford Files." His character, Lance White, received the credit for solving most of Rockford's cases.

This was one of the first shows of the '80s to deal seriously with bad memories of the Vietnam War. Magnum and all his buddies were vets of that conflict. Other shows to do the same included "Airwolf."

John Hillerman (Jonathan Higgins, III) had to put on a fake accent every week.

THE MAN FROM U.N.C.L.E.

Robert Vaugh (Napoleon Solo) was more than an Academy award- nominated actor, he was also a political activist. While making the show he wrote his dissertation for a Ph.D. in political science about McCarthy-era black-listing. He spoke out against the Vietnam War, and he was a close friend of Robert Kennedy.

When the show began, nobody - not even the producers - knew what U.N.C.L.E. stood for. The name had been chosen because it sounded funny. After several months the producers had been swamped with letters demanding to know U.N.C.L.E.'s full name. The producers quickly thought up a name for their crime-fighting organization: United Network Command for Law Enforcement.

The show was incredibly popular among college students. The show had awful ratings until the holiday seasons when college kids came home from school.

Many of the show's plots revolved around

the guns used by Napoleon and his partner Illya Kuryakin (David McCallum). Five guns were designed specifically for the show. The stars received 60,000 fan letters each month, and the guns received 2,000.

The show was highly controversial for its pairing of American spies and Russian spies together in a single organization. But producers insisted on this, in hopes of showing a peaceful resolution to the Cold War. David McCallum initially received many nasty letters for playing a Russian, but teenage girls who watched the show soon fell in love with him, and their letters became more positive.

Every episode was titled "The...Affair." Some of the more interesting titles included: "The Concrete Overcoat Affair" and "The Sort of Do-It-Yourself Dreadful Affair."

The evil organization that opposed U.N.C.L.E. was called THRUSH. It's name didn't stand for anything either.

Most memorable episode: bad guys try to drain Napoleon Solo's blood in order to revive Hitler's corpse.

THE MARY TYLER MOORE SHOW

This show won more Emmy awards than any other show in TV history. The only actor on the show not to win an Emmy was Gavin MacLeod (Murray), but he went on to great success in "The Love Boat."

This was one of the first shows in TV history in which a woman had complete creative control. Mary Tyler Moore not only starred in the show, but she created it and owned many of the rights to it. In order to make the show fresh and new, she decided to be a career-minded woman rather than a housewife, another first for TV.

Ted Knight played Ted Baxter, the moronic newscaster. After a while he became weary of playing such a dope, so the producers agreed to expand his character.

In 1959 Mary Tyler Moore got a part in a prime time show called "Richard Diamond." She played a telephone operator, and the audience only got to see her legs. She then moved on to playing the wife in "The Dick Van Dyke Show," which made her famous.

As good as ratings were for "The Mary Tyler Moore Show," the ratings for its two spin-offs, "Rhoda" and "Phyllis" were even higher. Both of those shows made it into the top ten.

The only character not to lose his job in the final episode of the show was Ted Baxter.

Famous episode: Mary's friend dies while dressed as a clown. Everyone thinks it's funny, except her. She feels horrible and can't understand why everyone thinks it's a laughing matter. But when she finally gets to the funeral, the humor of the situation finally hits her, and she cannot control her laughter.

Georgette (Georgia Engel) wears a plaid dress when she gets married to Ted Baxter. Plaid is Ted's favorite color.

Famous lines: "Oh, Mr. Grant," and "I HATE spunk!"

M*A*S*H

The show received very poor reviews and ratings during its first season, but the network stuck behind it. "M*A*S*H" eventually became such a success that it lasted for eleven seasons, nearly four times as long as the actual Korean War.

Alan Alda was very reluctant to play Hawkeye Pierce. He didn't accept the role until the day before rehearsals began.

Gary Burghoff (Radar O'Reilly) was the only actor to appear in the movie and the show.

The final episode was watched by more viewers than any other telecast in history.

Alan Alda's father, an actor who once guest starred on the show, wanted his son to be a doctor.

Richard Hooker, the author of the novel, hated the show. He was a hardline conservative, and it was never his intention to spawn a work with anti-war sentiments.

This was one of the first TV shows to feature true character development. Hot lips loosened up, Hawkeye stopped chasing women, and Frank Burns went insane.

Many of the story ideas were based on events that happened to Korean War veterans.

Many of the characters came and went as the show progressed. Colonel Henry Blake was killed off when MacLean Stevenson, the actor who played him, decided that he hated the working conditions on the outdoor sets.

One of Mike Farrell's (B.J. Hunnicut) first roles was as a bellhop in the hit movie *The Graduate*.

David Ogden Stiers (Charles Emerson Winchester, III) now performs Shakespeare on stage and conducts orchestras.

Most of the actors hoped the show would go on the air without a laugh-track. They got their wish, to a certain extent: the show never featured any laughter during the operating room scenes.

MIAMI VICE

This show was created when a network executive came up with the idea "Hill Street MTV."

The show was almost moved to a new city and changed to "San Diego Vice" in an attempt to break a strike by the Teamsters who drove the production trucks.

It was almost cancelled, but it was saved by a letter-writing campaign from fans.

The mayor of Miami hated the show because he felt it painted a poor picture of his city. But he changed his mind when tourism suddenly boomed.

Memorable character: Elvis, the alligator who swallowed a clock.

The show's soundtrack was comprised of the most popular songs of the '80s.

THE MONKEES

The band in this show was fabricated by the network. None of them could even play their own instruments. The network wanted to cash in on the success of the Beatles' films *A Hard Day's Night* and *Help*. The show won 2 Emmies for best comedy.

The Monkees "played" in concert as well as appearing on their show. One of their most famous opening acts was Jimi Hendrix. None of the audience members were interested in him, however, so he quit the tour.

Their albums all became huge hits. Their first two albums were #1 for a total of over thirty weeks. They only had a 25 percent royalty on the albums, as opposed to their producer, who had 15 percent.

The Monkees received 200,000 letters from fans each month.

John Lennon loved the show. He compared the Monkees to the Marx Brothers.

Davy Jones had trained to be a jockey, but he was slightly too heavy. He moved from England to the U.S. in hopes of becoming an actor. He was drafted during the Vietnam War but did not have to go because he financially supported his father.

Mike Nesmith took up guitar as a means of physical therapy for his hand, which had been injured in a fire cracker accident. His mother invented Liquid Paper, and he inherited twenty-five million dollars from her. He was one of the creators of MTV.

Peter Tork was recommended to the producers by his friend Stephen Stills (who was a member of Buffalo Springfield and Crosby, Stills, and Nash). Stills had auditioned to be in the group.

Mickey Dolenz studied architecture in case he didn't make it in show business. He was the only member of the group who had starred in a TV show. As a child, he had played an orphan in "Circus Boy."

THE ODD COUPLE

This show was based on a hit movie which was based on a hit play. The show was never a hit.

The show did not come to an end because of its poor ratings. Rather, the cast members simply grew tired of their roles and decided to call it quits.

Despite the fact that Tony Randall (Felix Ungar) had performed in the play "The Odd Couple," he was very reluctant to star in the TV show. His film career was finally taking off, and he did not want to threaten it.

Jack Klugman was not the producer's first choice for the part of Oscar Madison, the slobbish sports writer. He wanted Mickey Rooney to play the role.

The show won three Emmies. Klugman won two for his performances, and Randall won one.

Some network executives felt the show had poor ratings because they thought it was about two gay men. When the producer discovered this, he became infuriated and sent them film clips in which Randall and Klugman pretended to be gay. The executives almost fainted because he pretended that these were scenes from the following week's episode.

The situation of two divorced men living with each other was inspired by actual events in the life of the playwright's brother.

Penny Marshall (of "Laverne and Shirley" fame) played Oscar's secretary, Myrna Turner. She was the producer's sister, but that was not the reason for her playing the part. It was actually Jack Klugman who insisted that she be cast after having worked with her before. She is now an acclaimed film director.

Memorable moments: Felix making honking sounds because of his sinus problems, and Oscar spraying furniture polish into Felix's soup.

Memorable line: "Oscar, Oscar, Oscar."

THE ROCKFORD FILES

Despite rave reviews from audiences and critics, all of which stressed the show's humanity and sensitvity, the PTA spoke out against it because of its violence.

Jim Rockford was the first TV private eye who didn't carry a gun.

The producer created the character of Jim Rockford to appear as a guest investigator in a short-lived detective show named "Toma." A writers' strike had thrown that show completely off-schedule, and to make up time several episodes had to be filmed simultaneously. When the producer showed the Rockford episode to the network, they hated it. But one of the other networks agreed to buy the character, and "The Rockford Files" was born.

Stuart Margolin was an unusual choice to play Angel Martin, the slimy con-man. His only major previous experience had been in the sitcom "Love, American Style." But Margolin did such a good job that he won two Emmy awards.

The network that ran the show was very nervous about Rockford's unusual sense of humor. They wanted him to be more like Jack Lord on "Hawaii Five-O." When they attempted to make changes to the show, James Garner (Rockford) threatened to walk off. The network never disturbed the show again.

Some regular guest stars who went on to greater success included Rita Moreno and Tom Selleck.

James Garner became one of the most popular actors of the 1970s, due not only to his role in "The Rockford Files," but also to his appearances in Polaroid commercials. He left the show in 1980 when a back injury from a car stunt made it difficult for him to act.

Noah Beery ("Rocky" Rockford) had previously starred in movies with such film greats as John Wayne and Spencer Tracy. But he had also starred with such TV not-so-greats as Mickey Dolenz (of "Monkees" fame) in "Circus Boy."

This was James Garner's first series in which he did not play a cowboy.

SATURDAY NIGHT LIVE

This is the highest rated late night show of all time. It was the first show targeted directly at the baby boomer audience. It marked a return to live TV, as well as introducing America to dozens of hip new comedians.

On average, the sales of a rock group's album rises by over 250,000 copies during the month in which a band appears as musical guest on "Saturday Night Live."

The salary of the show's original cast (The Not Ready For Prime Time Players) was a mere $750 each per week.

One-third of the initial writers for "Saturday Night Live" got their jobs straight out of college.

Producers had their doubts about hiring John Belushi for the show. Everyone loved him (how else could one react to the Samurai Warrior, the Killer Bee, Joe Cocker, and Joliet Jake?), but they were nervous that he was not disciplined enough for live TV.

Bill Murray broke into comedy when he found himself without a job after being released from jail. He had been arrested on his twenty-first birthday for possession of eight pounds of marijuana.

Dan Ackroyd was one of the last performers hired onto the original cast. He was given such short notice that he had to commute between his home in Canada and the studio in New York for much of the first season.

Eddie Murphy made his first appearance on the show at the age of nineteen. He played Little Richard Simmons in his first sketch. Two short years later he was a movie star.

Billy Crystal was scheduled to perform a stand-up routine on the first episode of the show, but he was dropped because the show ran too long. It was a dream come true for him several years later when he was invited to be a regular on the show.

Famous lines: "Isn't that special," "I'm Chevy Chase and you're not," and "You look marvelous."

THE SMOTHERS BROTHERS COMEDY HOUR

This was one of the most controversial shows of the 1960s and '70s. Tom and Dick Smothers frequently defied efforts by the network to censor their show; as a result, the press battles concerning the making of the show were often just as entertaining as the show itself.

In order to strengthen their power over the show, the network frequently moved them from one time-slot to another. This played havoc with the show's ratings.

Tom and Dick Smothers had been successful night club entertainers, Tom playing the guitar and Dick playing the bass. They sang humorous and socially aware folk songs. The network felt the two would make excellent hosts for a variety show.

The show launched the careers of many entertainers, such as Glen Campbell and Mac Davis. It also jumpstarted the careers of blacklisted entertainers Joan Baez and Pete Seeger.

Pat Paulsen (a regular on the show) campaigned for the Presidency throughout 1968 on the show. His campaign apparently affected the election, as many fans voted for him, resulting in one of the closest election victories in history. Hubert Humphrey actually blamed Paulsen for his loss at the polls.

David Steinberg, a guest on the show, once delivered a mock sermon considered so blasphemous by clergy members across the country, that he had to make a public apology.

Tom sang in the chorus of "Give Peace a Chance," by John Lennon.

STAR TREK

William Shatner turned down the role of "Dr. Kildare" in order to play James T. Kirk.

Although "Star Trek" has become a huge hit in syndication, spawning movies and a spin-off, the show was never very popular during its original run.

The original pilot for the show featured a more pensive captain named Christopher Pike and an entirely different crew. The only character to remain was Mr. Spock, who became a big hit with teenage viewers.

The show consistently grappled with serious issues, such as racism. It was the first show in the history of American TV to show an interracial kiss.

The character Chekov, a Russian navigator, was added after reporters for the Russian newspaper *Pravda* pointed out that their countrymen were, after all, the first men in space.

Nichelle Nichols (Uhura) considered leaving

the show because she didn't have a big enough part, but she decided to stay when Dr. Martin Luther King, Jr. told her that her character was a positive inspiration to young African American women.

George Takei (Mr. Sulu) spent part of World War II in a Japanese internment camp.

William Shatner used to exercise hard before the start of each season, but he would stop when filming began. As a result, his stomach would grow quite noticeably as the season wore on.

The original title of the show was "Star Track."

Leonard Nimoy protested vehemently against his character having pointy ears.

The show featured many guest stars who went on to great success. Some episodes even featured the likes of Joan Collins and Ricardo Montalban.

The Enterprise's five year mission was cut short by poor ratings. The show only lasted three seasons.

TAXI

The entire cast of "Taxi" received a Golden Globe award nomination in 1979.

Christopher Loyd (Reverend Jim Ignatausky) and Danny DeVito (Louie DePalma) were both successful film actors. The two had worked together previously on the acclaimed *One Flew Over the Cuckoo's Nest*.

Judd Hirsch (Alex Reiger) hated TV and wanted to act on Broadway. But after repeated calls from producers he finally decided to accept the part.

"Taxi" was moved from one network to another in 1982. Despite such a drastic event, the show continued to be a success.

Andy Kaufman (Latka Gravis) was so strange in real life that he had been seeing a psychiatrist since he was four years old. His first big success came from occasional appearances on "Saturday Night Live."

Marilu Henner was an acclaimed Broadway

actress. She had won rave reviews for her performance in "Grease."

Rhea Perlman (of "Cheers" fame) had occasional appearances as one of Louie's (Danny DeVito) girlfriends. The two had lived together for eleven years, and they got married during one of their lunchbreaks.

Judd Hirsch and Danny DeVito had appeared in a play together prior to "Taxi." DeVito had played Hirsch's dog.

Andy Kaufman's performances of various characters in his stand-up routines were so intense that he bordered on having a split-personality. The producers of "Taxi" even signed one of his alter egos to an independent contract in case his personality ever truly split.

"Taxi" was an attempt to speak out against the budding materialism at the end of the '70s and throughout the '80s. Alex Rieger was supposed to have given up a successful corporate career in order to become a cab driver, because he found his white-collar life so unethical.

THE TWILIGHT ZONE

This is perhaps the only show in history ever to have an episode win an Academy award. The final episode was a short film made in France, thereby qualifying it for an Oscar. It was also the only episode ever to be seen on another series; it was also shown on "Alfred Hitchcock Presents."

Rod Serling loved to seek out new talent. When he started the show, he invited any viewers to submit a script. He was flooded with over 14,000 scripts, and he actually got around to reading 500 of them. But only 2 were any good, and he couldn't use them because they didn't fit the format of the show.

The show never had very good ratings, but it could always find advertisers due to its high quality.

Rod Serling thought he had invented the name "Twilight Zone." But he soon found out that it was a name used by Air Force pilots to describe the moment when a plane loses sight of the horizon while landing.

Despite having intense stage fright, Rod Serling insisted that he introduce and conclude each episode. The producers had wanted Orson Welles to narrate.

Serling was a prolific and award-winning writer. Two of his more famous works include "Requiem for a Heavyweight" and *Planet of the Apes*.

Many of the show's guest stars went on to great fame. These included Jack Klugman, William Shatner, Burgess Meredith, Dick York, Roddy McDowell, Cliff Robertson, Lee Marvin, Jonathan Winters, and Robert Redford.

Serling quit his job as a writer for "Playhouse 90" during the 1950s because sponsors had too much control over story content (sometimes even more than producers). An insurance company that sponsored the show, for example, refused to let one of the central characters commit suicide. Serling decided to create "The Twilight Zone" because he felt it would be more difficult for sponsors to censor a fantasy show.

YOU BET YOUR LIFE

This show saved Groucho Marx's career. His radio show was faltering, and he needed a forum in which he could improvise.

Julius Henry Marx never wanted to go into show business. His childhood dream had been to become a doctor. He was nicknamed Groucho because he was always so bitter.

One night a contestant on the show named Bill Blatty won $10,000. He was thrilled, because all of a sudden he had enough money to quit work and write a novel. He went on to write the bestseller "The Exorcist."

A housewife who dreamed of being a comedienne was once a contestant on the show. She came onto the stage wearing a sack dress, a style so new that no one had ever worn one on TV before. Her name was Phyllis Diller.

Groucho felt bad whenever he had to send a player away empty-handed. He decided that everyone should have the opportunity to win a consolation prize if they could answer an incredibly simple question. As a result, anyone who lost was asked, "Who is buried in Grant's tomb?"

"You Bet Your Life" was the most popular game show ever to air during prime time.

If a contestant ever said the "secret word," a stuffed duck would fall from the rafters holding a check. Sometimes Groucho played a trick on contestants and had a beautiful model descend with the check. He once even had Harpo Marx climb down holding the check.

In 1973 NBC started burning the negatives of old films in order to clear space in their vaults for newer shows. Fifteen episodes of "You Bet Your Life" were destroyed, along with most of the Jack Paar episodes of "The Tonight Show." But the producer of "You Bet Your Life" was able to step in and save the remaining 235 episodes.

Producers of the show decided they wanted to see Groucho in a mustache again (he had stopped wearing his grease mustache since his last film). He refused to put grease on his face again, but he agreed to grow a real one.

APPENDIX

EMMY AWARD
BEST COMEDY SERIES

1992 "Murphy Brown"
1991 "Cheers"
1990 "Murphy Brown"
1989 "Cheers"
1988 "The Wonder Years"
1987 "The Golden Girls"
1986 "The Golden Girls"
1985 "The Cosby Show"
1984 "Cheers"
1983 "Cheers"
1982 "Barney Miller"
1981 "Taxi"
1980 "Taxi"
1979 "Taxi"
1978 "All in the Family"
1977 "The Mary Tyler Moore Show"
1976 "The Mary Tyler Moore Show"
1975 "The Mary Tyler Moore Show"
1974 "M*A*S*H"
1973 "All in the Family"
1972 "All in the Family"
1971 "All in the Family"
1970 "My World and Welcome to it"

EMMY AWARD
BEST DRAMA SERIES

1992   "Northern Exposure"
1991   "LA Law"
1990   "LA Law"
1989   "LA Law"
1988   "Thirtysomething"
1987   "LA Law"
1986   "Cagney & Lacey"
1985   "Cagney & Lacey"
1984   "Hill Street Blues"
1983   "Hill Street Blues"
1982   "Hill Street Blues"
1981   "Hill Street Blues"
1980   "Lou Grant"
1979   "Lou Grant"
1978   "The Rockford Files"
1977   "Upstairs, Downstairs"
1976   "Police Story"
1975   "Upstairs, Downstairs"
1974   "Upstairs, Downstairs"
1973   "The Waltons"
1972   "Elizabeth R"
1971   "The Senator"
1970   "Marcus Welby, MD"

EMMY AWARD
BEST COMEDY ACTOR

1992   Craig T. Nelson, "Coach"
1991   Burt Reynolds, "Evening Shade"
1990   Ted Danson, "Cheers"
1989   Richard Mulligan, "Empty Nest"
1988   Michael J. Fox, "Family Ties"
1987   Michael J. Fox, "Family Ties"
1986   Michael J. Fox, "Family Ties"
1985   Robert Guillaume, "Benson"
1984   John Ritter, "Three's Company"
1983   Judd Hirsch, "Taxi"
1982   Alan Alda, "M*A*S*H"
1981   Judd Hirsch, "Taxi"
1980   Richard Mulligan, "Soap"
1979   Carroll O'Connor, "All in the Family"
1978   Carroll O'Connor, "All in the Family"
1977   Carroll O'Connor, "All in the Family"
1976   Jack Albertson, "Chico and the Man"
1975   Tony Randall, "The Odd Couple"
1974   Alan Alda, "M*A*S*H"
1973   Jack Klugman, "The Odd Couple"
1972   Carroll O'Connor, "All in the Family"
1971   Jack Klugman, "The Odd Couple"
1970   William Windom, "My World and
        Welcome to it"

EMMY AWARD
BEST COMEDY ACTRESS

1992 Candice Bergen, "Murphy Brown"
1991 Kirstie Alley, "Cheers"
1990 Candice Bergen, "Murphy Brown"
1989 Candice Bergen, "Murphy Brown"
1988 Beatrice Arthur, "The Golden Girls"
1987 Rue McClanahan, "The Golden Girls"
1986 Betty White, "The Golden Girls"
1985 Jane Curtin, "Kate and Allie"
1984 Jane Curtin, "Kate and Allie"
1983 Shelley Long, "Cheers"
1982 Carol Kane, "Taxi"
1981 Isabel Sanford, "The Jeffersons"
1980 Cathryn Damon, "Soap"
1979 Ruth Gordon, "Taxi"
1978 Jean Stapleton, "All in the Family"
1977 Beatrice Arthur, "Maude"
1976 Mary Tyler Moore, "The Mary Tyler
      Moore Show"
1975 Valerie Harper, "Rhoda"
1974 Mary Tyler Moore, "The MTM Show"
1973 Mary Tyler Moore, "The MTM Show"
1972 Jean Stapleton, "All in the Family"
1971 Jean Stapleton, "All in the Family"
1970 Hope Lange, "The Ghost and Mrs. Muir"

EMMY AWARD
BEST DRAMA ACTOR

1992   Richard Dysart, "L.A. Law"
1991   James Earl Jones, "Gabriel's Fire"
1990   Peter Falk, "Columbo"
1989   Carroll O'Connor, "In the Heat of the Night"
1988   Richard Kiley, "A Year in the Life"
1987   Bruce Willis, "Moonlighting"
1986   William Daniels, "St. Elsewhere"
1985   William Daniels, "St. Elsewhere"
1984   Tom Selleck, "Magnum, PI"
1983   Ed Flanders, "St. Elsewhere"
1982   Daniel J. Travanti, "Hill Street Blues"
1981   Daniel J. Travanti, "Hill Street Blues"
1980   Ed Asner, "Lou Grant"
1979   Ron Leibman, "Kaz"
1978   Ed Asner, "Lou Grant"
1977   James Garner, "The Rockford Files"
1976   Peter Falk, "Columbo"
1975   Robert Blake, "Baretta"
1974   Telly Savalas, "Kojak"
1973   Richard Thomas, "The Waltons"
1972   Peter Falk, "Columbo"
1971   Hal Holbrook, "The Senator"
1970   Robert Young, "Marcus Welby, MD"

EMMY AWARD
BEST DRAMA ACTRESS

1992   Dana Delaney, "China Beach"
1991   Patricia Wettig, "Thirtysomething"
1990   Patricia Wettig, "Thirtysomething"
1989   Dana Delaney, "China Beach"
1988   Tyne Daly, "Cagney & Lacey"
1987   Sharon Gless, "Cagney & Lacey"
1986   Sharon Gless, "Cagney & Lacey"
1985   Tyne Daly, "Cagney & Lacey"
1984   Tyne Daly, "Cagney & Lacey"
1983   Tyne Daly, "Cagney & Lacey"
1982   Michael Learned, "Nurse"
1981   Barbara Babcock, "Hill Street Blues"
1980   Barbara Bel Geddes, "Dallas"
1979   Mariette Hartley, "Incredible Hulk"
1978   Sada Thompson, "Family"
1977   Lindsay Wagner, "The Bionic Woman"
1976   Michael Learned, "The Waltons"
1975   Jean Marsh, "Upstairs, Downstairs"
1974   Michael Learned, "The Waltons"
1973   Michael Learned, "The Waltons"
1972   Glenda Jackson, "Elizabeth R"
1971   Susan Hampshire, "The First Churchills"
1970   Susan Hampshire, "The Forsythe Saga"

EMMY AWARD
BEST INFORMATIONAL SERIES

1992 "MGM: When The Lion Roars"
1991 "The Civil War"
1990 "Smithsonian World"
1989 "Nature"
1988 "Buster Keaton: A Hard Act to Follow:
       American Masters"
1987 "Smithsonian World"
1986 "Laurence Olivier—A Life"
1985 "The Living Planet: A Portrait of
       Earth"
1984 "A Walk Through the Twentieth
       Century"
1983 "The Barbara Walters Specials"
1982 "Creativity with Bill Moyers"
1981 "Steve Allen's Meeting of Minds"
1980 "The Body Human: The Magic Sense"
1979 "Scared Straight"
1978 "The Body Human"

THEME SONGS THAT MADE "BILLBOARD" MAGAZINE'S TOP 20 SINGLES CHART

"Angie": *Different Worlds*, Maureen McGovern, #18

"Baretta": *Keep Your Eye on the Sparrow*, Rhythm Heritage, #20

"Bonanza": *Bonanza*, Al Caiola, #19

"Dr. Kildare": *Three Stars Will Shine Tonight*, Richard Chamberlain, #10

"Dragnet": *Dragnet*, Ray Anthony Orchestra, #3

"The Greatest American Hero": *Believe it or Not*, Joey Scarbury, #2

"Happy Days": *Happy Days*, Pratt & McClain, #5

"Hawaii Five-O": *Hawaii Five-O*, The Ventures, #4

"Hill Street Blues": *Hill Street Blues*, Mike Post with Larry Carlton, #10

"Makin' It": *Makin' It*, David Naughton, #5

"Miami Vice": *Miami Vice*, Jan Hammer, #1

"Peter Gunn": *Peter Gunn*, Ray Anthony Orchestra, #8

"The Rockford Files": *The Rockford Files*, Mike Post, #10

"S.W.A.T.": *S.W.A.T.*, Rhythm Heritage, #1

"Secret Agent": *Secret Agent Man*, Johnny Rivers, #3

"Welcome Back, Kotter": *Welcome Back*, John Sebastian, #1

"Zorro": *Zorro*, The Chordettes, #17

TOP TEN SHOWS
BY NIELSON RATING

1991
1) Cheers
2) 60 Minutes
3) Roseanne
4) A Different World
5) The Cosby Show
6) Murphy Brown
7) Empty Nest
8) America's Funniest Home Videos
9) Monday Night Football
10) The Golden Girls

1990
1) The Cosby Show
2) Roseanne
3) Cheers
4) A Different World
5) America's Funniest Home Videos
6) The Golden Girls
7) 60 Minutes
8) The Wonder Years
9) Empty Nest
10) Monday Night Football

1989
1) The Cosby Show
2) Roseanne
3) A Different World
4) Cheers
5) 60 Minutes
6) The Golden Girls
7) Who's the Boss?
8) Murder, She Wrote
9) Empty Nest
10) Anything But Love

1988
1) The Cosby Show
2) A Different World
3) Cheers
4) The Golden Girls
5) Growing Pains
6) Who's the Boss?
7) Night Court
8) 60 Minutes
9) Murder, She Wrote
10) Alf

1987
1) The Cosby Show
2) Family Ties
3) Cheers
4) Murder, She Wrote
5) The Golden Girls
6) 60 Minutes
7) Night Court
8) Growing Pains
9) Moonlighting
10) Who's the Boss?

1986
1) The Cosby Show
2) Family Ties
3) Murder, She Wrote
4) 60 Minutes
5) Cheers
6) Dallas
7) Dynasty
8) The Golden Girls
9) Miami Vice
10) Who's the Boss?

1985
1) Dynasty
2) Dallas
3) The Cosby Show
4) 60 Minutes
5) Family Ties
6) The A-Team
7) Simon & Simon
8) Murder, She Wrote
9) Knots Landing
10) Falcon Crest

1984
1) Dallas
2) 60 Minutes
3) Dynasty
4) The A-Team
5) Simon & Simon
6) Magnum, PI
7) Falcon Crest
8) Kate & Allie
9) Hotel
10) Cagney & Lacey

1983
1) 60 Minutes
2) Dallas
3) M*A*S*H
4) Magnum, PI
5) Dynasty
6) Three's Company
7) Simon & Simon
8) Falcon Crest
9) The Love Boat
10) The A-Team

1982
1) Dallas
2) 60 Minutes
3) The Jeffersons
4) Three's Company
5) Alice
6) The Dukes of Hazard
7) Too Close for Comfort
8) ABC Monday Night Movie
9) M*A*S*H
10) One Day at a Time

1981
1) Dallas
2) The Dukes of Hazard
3) 60 Minutes
4) M*A*S*H
5) The Love Boat
6) The Jeffersons
7) Alice
8) House Calls
9) Three's Company
10) Little House on the Prairie

1980
1) 60 Minutes
2) Three's Company
3) That's Incredible
4) Alice
5) M*A*S*H
6) Dallas
7) Flo
8) The Jeffersons
9) The Dukes of Hazzard
10) One Day at a Time

1979
1) Laverne & Shirley
2) Three's Company
3) Mork & Mindy
4) Happy Days
5) Angie
6) 60 Minutes
7) M*A*S*H
8) The Ropers
9) All in the Family
10) Taxi

1978
1) Laverne & Shirley
2) Happy Days
3) Three's Company
4) 60 Minutes
5) Charlie's Angels
6) All in the Family
7) Little House on the Prairie
8) Alice
9) M*A*S*H
10) One Day at a Time

1977

1) Happy Days
2) Laverne & Shirley
3) ABC Monday Night Movie
4) M*A*S*H
5) Charlie's Angels
6) The Big Event
7) The Six Million Dollar Man
8) ABC Sunday Night Movie
9) Baretta
10) One Day at a Time

1976

1) All in the Family
2) Rich Man, Poor Man
3) Laverne & Shirley
4) Maude
5) The Bionic Woman
6) Phyllis
7) Sanford and Son
8) Rhoda
9) The Six Million Dollar Man
10) ABC Monday Night Movie

1975

1) All in the Family
2) Sanford and Son
3) Chico and the Man
4) The Jeffersons
5) M*A*S*H
6) Rhoda
7) Good Times
8) The Waltons
9) Maude
10) Hawaii Five-O

1974

1) All in the Family
2) The Waltons
3) Sanford and Son
4) M*A*S*H
5) Hawaii Five-O
6) Maude
7) Kojak
8) The Sonny and Cher Comedy Hour
9) The Mary Tyler Moore Show
10) Cannon

1973

1) All in the Family
2) Sanford and Son
3) Hawaii Five-O
4) Maude
5) Bridget Loves Bernie
6) The NBC Sunday Mystery Movie
7) The Mary Tyler Moore Show
8) Gunsmoke
9) The Wonderful World of Disney
10) Ironside

1972

1) All in the Family
2) The Flip Wilson Show
3) Marcus Welby, MD
4) Gunsmoke
5) ABC Movie of the Week
6) Sanford and Son
7) Mannix
8) Funny Face
9) Adam 12
10) The Mary Tyler Moore Show

1971

1) Marcus Welby, MD
2) The Flip Wilson Show
3) Here's Lucy
4) Ironside
5) Gunsmoke
6) ABC Movie of the Week
7) Hawaii Five-O
8) Medical Center
9) Bonanza
10) The FBI

1970

1) Rowan & Martin's Laugh-In
2) Gunsmoke
3) Bonanza
4) Mayberry, RFD
5) Family Affair
6) Here's Lucy
7) The Red Skelton Hour
8) Marcus Welby, MD
9) Walt Disney's Wonderful World of Color
10) The Doris Day Show